Jackie Robinson
Hero and Athlete

by SUZANNE SLADE

illustrated by THOMAS SPENCE

Special thanks to our advisers for their expertise:

John Vernon, Historical Consultant
Clarksville, Maryland

Terry Flaherty, Ph.D., Professor of English
Minnesota State University, Mankato

Editor: Shelly Lyons
Designer: Abbey Fitzgerald and Hilary Wacholz
Page Production: Michelle Biedscheid
Art Director: Nathan Gassman
Associate Managing Editor: Christianne Jones
The illustrations in this book were created with acrylics and ink.
Photo Credit: Library of Congress, page 3

Picture Window Books
5115 Excelsior Boulevard, Suite 232
Minneapolis, MN 55416
877-845-8392
www.picturewindowbooks.com

Printed in the United States of America.

 All books published by Picture Window Books
are manufactured with paper containing at least
10 percent post-consumer waste.

Library of Congress Cataloging-in-Publication Data
Slade, Suzanne.
Jackie Robinson : hero and athlete / by Suzanne Slade ; illustrated by Thomas Spence.
p. cm. — (Biographies)
Includes index.
ISBN 978-1-4048-3978-6 (library binding)
1. Robinson, Jackie, 1919-1972—Juvenile literature. 2. Baseball players—United
States—Biography—Juvenile literature.
3. African American baseball players—Biography—Juvenile literature. I. Spence, Tom,
1980- ill. II. Title.
GV865.R6S63 2008
796.357092—dc22
[B]   2007032883

In the 1940s, people of different races did not always have equal rights. Jackie Robinson hoped to change that. He became the first black Major League Baseball player in 1947. Jackie was brave, kind, and full of team spirit. With these qualities, he played well and helped bring blacks and whites in the United States closer together.

This is the story of

Jackie Robinson.

home when Jackie was a baby. Jackie's mother, Mallie Robinson, raised her five children alone. When Jackie was only 1 year old, his family moved to California. His mother hoped to find a good-paying job there.

Only a few black families lived near Jackie's new home in Pasadena, California. Many of Jackie's white neighbors were mean to him because he was black. Jackie's mother taught him to be kind to others, even when they treated him unfairly. But she also told her children to stand up for their own rights.

6

Growing up, Jackie discovered he had talent in many sports. During college at UCLA, he played football, basketball, and baseball. He was also a track star.

In 1942, Jackie was called into the Army and helped the United States fight World War II (1939–1945). During his time in the service, Jackie saw that black and white soldiers were not treated the same. He grew tired of such unfairness, and he longed for change.

Jackie met a soldier who had played for an all-black professional baseball team in the Negro National League. The team was called the Kansas City Monarchs. In 1945, Jackie decided to try out for the Monarchs. With his great baseball skills, Jackie made the team and became its starting shortstop.

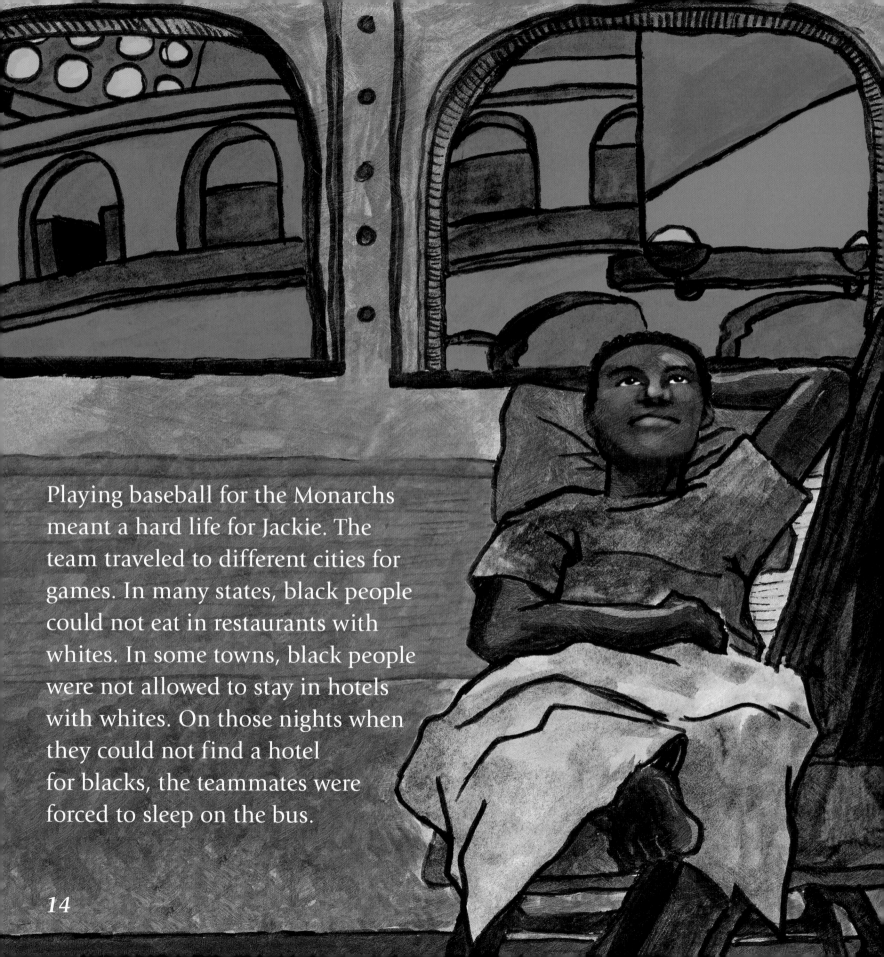

Playing baseball for the Monarchs meant a hard life for Jackie. The team traveled to different cities for games. In many states, black people could not eat in restaurants with whites. In some towns, black people were not allowed to stay in hotels with whites. On those nights when they could not find a hotel for blacks, the teammates were forced to sleep on the bus.

14

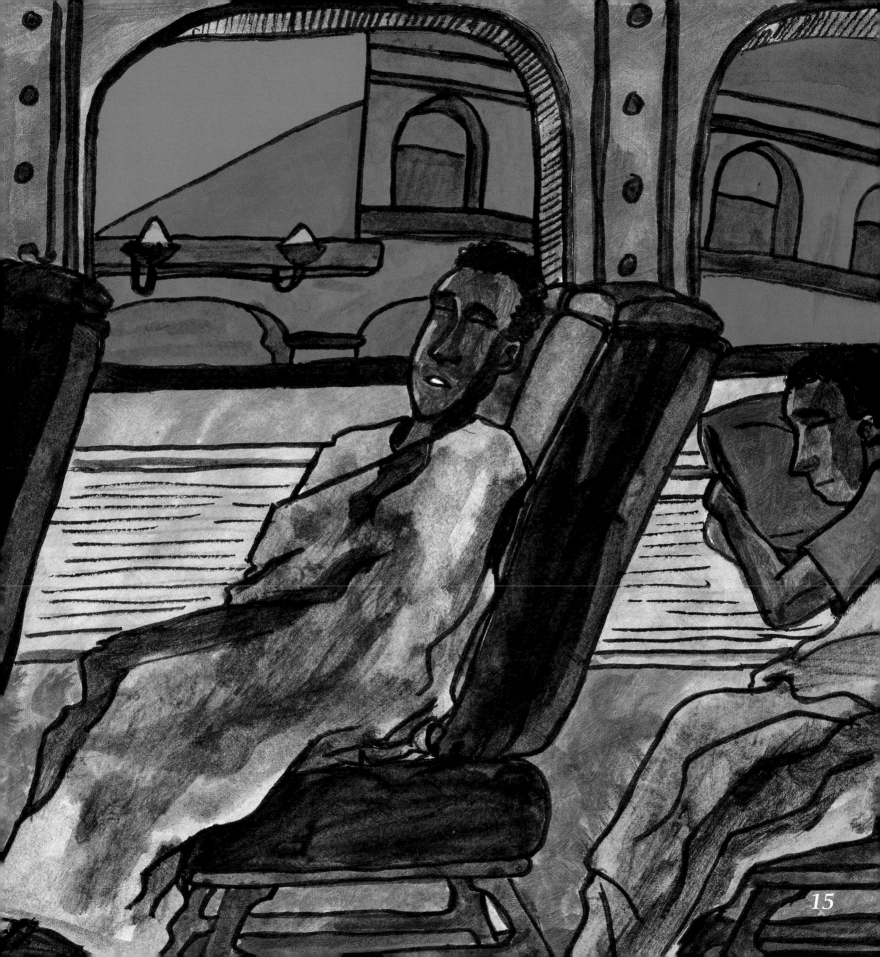

In 1947, Jackie was given the chance to stand up for blacks' rights and bring change to the United States. The Brooklyn Dodgers asked him to be the first black player on a Major League Baseball team. Although Jackie knew breaking this new ground would be difficult, he joined the team.

Many people were angry when Jackie joined the Dodgers. Some white fans threw things at him. People called him terrible names. Many white players disliked him, until they saw him play. Through it all, Jackie held his temper and played great baseball. Jackie's character and strength showed people that everyone should be treated the same.

19

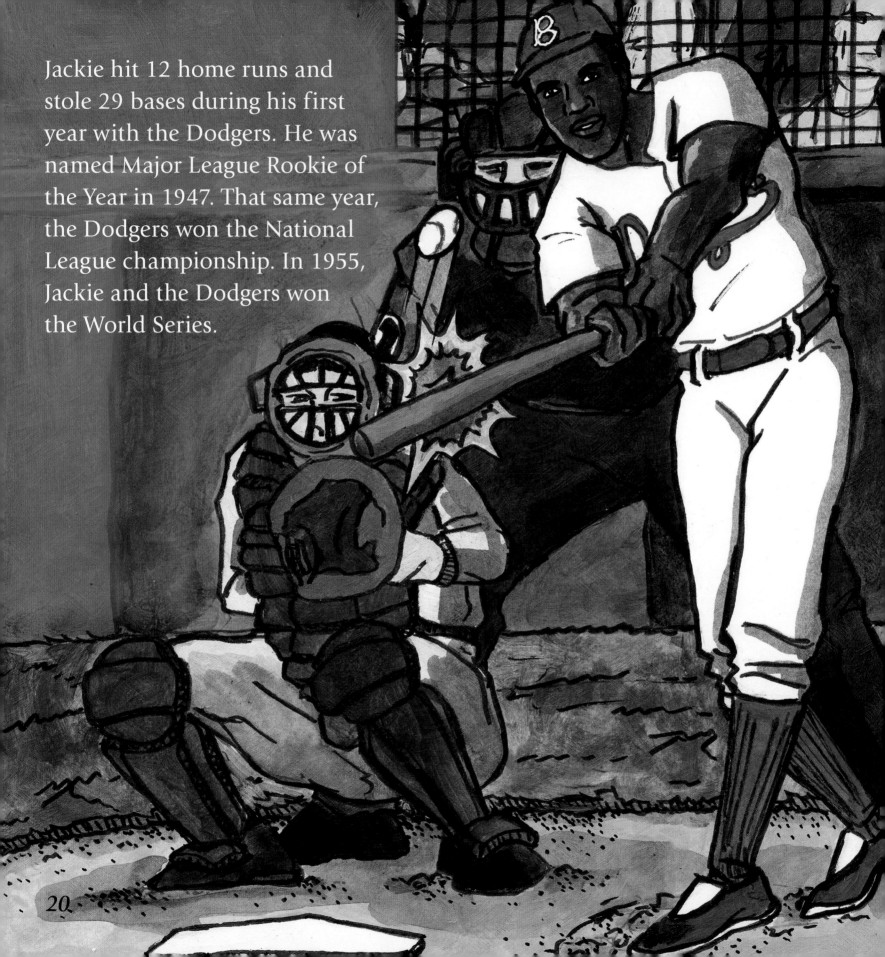

Jackie hit 12 home runs and stole 29 bases during his first year with the Dodgers. He was named Major League Rookie of the Year in 1947. That same year, the Dodgers won the National League championship. In 1955, Jackie and the Dodgers won the World Series.

Jackie cleared the way for other black players to join the Major Leagues. Jackie also proved that blacks and whites could do great things when they work together. Jackie continued to set an example for others until he died in 1972.

The Life of Jackie Robinson

1919	Born January 31 in Cairo, Georgia
1939	Began his studies at the University of California, Los Angeles
1942	Joined the U.S. Army
1945	Joined the Kansas City Monarchs
1946	Married Rachel Isum
1947	Played his first Major League game for the Brooklyn Dodgers
1949	Won the National League's batting title, stolen base crown, and the Most Valuable Player award
1962	Voted into the National Baseball Hall of Fame
1972	Died October 24 from a heart attack in Stanford, Connecticut
2005	Given the nation's highest honor, the Congressional Gold Medal

Did You Know?

~ Jackie married Rachel Isum, a woman he met at UCLA, in 1946. They had three children, named Jackie Jr., Sharon, and David.

~ Jackie co-wrote a book about his life called *Jackie Robinson: My Own Story* in 1948.

~ Jackie was an actor in a movie about his life called "The Jackie Robinson Story." The movie came out in 1950. It was the first full-length feature film about an African-American.

~ In 1970, Jackie started the Jackie Robinson Construction Company. This company built houses for families that did not have a lot of money.

~ In 1982, Jackie became the first Major League Baseball player to appear on a U.S. stamp. Additional stamps with Jackie's picture came out in 1997 and 2000.

~ In 1997, 50 years after Jackie played in his first Major League Baseball game, the number on Jackie's baseball uniform was retired in the Major Leagues. This meant that no new baseball players on any Major League team would be given his number, 42.

Glossary

Major League Baseball — a group of baseball teams that are made up of the best players in the United States

rookie — a player who is playing his first year on a team

UCLA — letters that stand for a college in California called University of California, Los Angeles

World Series — a group of games in which the two best baseball teams play against each other

World War II (1939–1945) — the war fought by the United States, Great Britain, France, and the Soviet Union against Germany, Japan, and Italy

23

To Learn More

More Books to Read

Glaser, Jason. *Jackie Robinson: Baseball's Great Pioneer.* Mankato, Minn.: Capstone Press, 2006.

Patrick, Denise Lewis. *Jackie Robinson, Strong Inside and Out.* New York: HarperCollins Children's Books, 2005.

Robinson, Sharon. *Promises to Keep: How Jackie Robinson Changed America.* New York: Scholastic Press, 2004.

Stout, Glenn. *Jackie Robinson.* New York: Little Brown, 2006.

On the Web

FactHound offers a safe, fun way to find Web sites related to topics in this book. All of the sites on FactHound have been researched by our staff.

1. Visit *www.facthound.com*

2. Type in this special code: 140483978X

3. Click on the FETCH IT button.

Your trusty FactHound will fetch the best sites for you!

Index

Look for all of the books in the Biographies series:

Abraham Lincoln: *Lawyer, President, Emancipator*

Albert Einstein: *Scientist and Genius*

Amelia Earhart: *Female Pioneer in Flight*

Benjamin Franklin: *Writer, Inventor, Statesman*

Booker T. Washington: *Teacher, Speaker, and Leader*

Cesar Chavez: *Champion and Voice of Farmworkers*

Frederick Douglass: *Writer, Speaker, and Opponent of Slavery*

George Washington: *Farmer, Soldier, President*

George Washington Carver: *Teacher, Scientist, and Inventor*

Harriet Tubman: *Hero of the Underground Railroad*

Jackie Robinson: *Hero and Athlete*

Marie Curie: *Prize-Winning Scientist*

Martha Washington: *First Lady of the United States*

Martin Luther King Jr.: *Preacher, Freedom Fighter, Peacemaker*

Pocahontas: *Peacemaker and Friend to the Colonists*

Sally Ride: *Astronaut, Scientist, Teacher*

Sojourner Truth: *Preacher for Freedom and Equality*

Susan B. Anthony: *Fighter for Freedom and Equality*

Thomas Edison: *Inventor, Scientist, and Genius*

Thomas Jefferson: *A Founding Father of the United States of America*